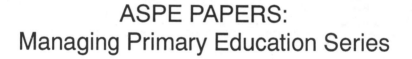
ASPE PAPERS:
Managing Primary Education Series

ASPE PAPER Number 3
Managing Access and Entitlement in Primary Education

Barbara MacGilchrist
Institute of Education
University of London

ASPE/Trentham Books

First published in 1992 by Trentham Books Limited

Trentham Books Limited
Westview House
734 London Road
Oakhill
Stoke-on-Trent
England ST4 5NP

British Library Cataloguing in Publication Data
A catalogue record for this book is available from the British Library.

ISBN: 0 948080 76 0

Designed and typeset by Trentham Print Design Ltd, Chester
and printed in Great Britain by Bemrose Shafron Ltd, Chester.

MANAGING PRIMARY EDUCATION

The ASPE papers comprise a series, published on behalf of the Association for the Study of Primary Education, in which major issues in primary education are analysed and implications for policy are drawn. The objectives of the papers are:

a.   to shift from the inevitably reactive stance imposed by the cycle of receiving and attempting to respond to documents from bodies like DES, SED, DENI, NCC, CCW and SEAC to a much more proactive position;

b.   to undertake work on central issues in primary education which are of more than transient interest and which might be seen to constitute part of the longer-term educational agenda;

The overall theme of the first series of ASPE papers is 'Managing Primary Education'. The working titles of the papers within this theme are as follows:

Managing Learning in the Primary Classroom

Managing Teachers' Time in Primary Schools

Managing Access and Entitlement in Primary Education

Managing Education in Smaller Primary Schools

Primary Teachers, Parents and Governors

Primary Teachers: Supply, Training and Professional Development.

As far as possible the papers reflect the particular aspirations of the Association: they are grounded in careful analysis and up-to-date evidence; they draw as appropriate on school, local, national and research perspectives and on the activities of regional branches and their local groups. This range of perspectives is combined with a serious attempt to crystallise conclusions and pointers for the future.

ASPE has deliberately chosen a set of issues which are of concern to policy-makers as well as practitioners. The Association wishes to target policy makers at DES, SED, DENI, NCC, CCW, SEAC, in LEAs, and elsewhere. It also intends to send copies to relevant members of the government and opposition parties.

The structure of the papers varies according to the theme and editors' preferences. However, the papers are intended to include:

i.   an identification of the central issues and challenges of the theme in question;

ii.   some contrasting examples of practice;

iii. reference to recent published study and research;

iv.   assessment of current strengths and weaknesses;

v.   indication of what needs to be done.

Although the papers will be published in a common format as ASPE papers, and will thus represent statements from the Association as a whole, they will also be very much the creations of their individual editors.

Managing Access and Entitlement in Primary Education

Barbara MacGilchrist
Institute of Education
University of London

SUMMARY

This paper argues that legislating for access and entitlement in primary education will not of itself ensure equality of educational opportunity for all children. Managing access and entitlement to the curriculum requires strategic management by all those concerned. This is a collective responsibility that should be perceived as a 'partnership for entitlement'. Improving the progress and attainment of all children as well as closing the achievement gap between the lowest and the highest achievers is a major challenge. Through an examination of notions of good primary practice and a review of the research literature, the paper concludes that schools and those who teach in them hold the master key to access and entitlement. To enable the key to be used to unlock the door to raising achievement requires the different partners — those within the school and those beyond the school gate — to take action in respect of policy decisions over which they can exercise direct control. This paper identifies practical strategies for managing access and entitlement and concludes by raising some concerns for the future.

In support of the main thrust of the argument developed within the paper ten key points are made:

● **Arguments about 'process' versus 'content'** in primary education are redundant and meaningless. Both are essential. It is the extent of the match between the learning process and the content to be learnt that will determine not just the quality of primary education on offer for the child but also the equality of opportunity for each child to learn. The teaching methods used by the teacher to ensure this match are all important.

● **There is a link between disadvantage and achievement,** with socio-economic inequality in particular a powerful determinant of differences in cognitive and educational attainment. This link can affect children's life chances and influence teachers' expectations of children's capacity to learn.

● The **involvement of parents** in the education of their own children is an important contributing factor.

● **Early rates of progress in reading, writing and mathematics** are very good predictors of later levels of attainment at age 7, 11 and 16, with the gap in achievement between different groups widening over time.

● **Recording academic achievement** needs to be done within the context of a broader record of achievement that includes pupil motivation and personal and social development.

● **Schools matter.** There is a growing amount of research evidence to demonstrate that despite background factors, schools can and do enhance the achievement of all pupils and some schools are much more effective than others at doing so. It is possible to identify factors related to progress and attainment that schools have it within their control to do something about. Recent studies demonstrate how schools can not only 'jack-up' achievement for all, but override disadvantage by narrowing the gap between the lowest and highest achieving groups.

● **Good quality nursery education** is a major factor in raising the achievement levels of disadvantaged children.

● Test results alone are misleading. Rates of pupil progress — the **value added** by the school — rather than summative snapshots are a good indicator of an effective school.

● **Managing access and entitlement in practice** within the school involves:

    i.   establishing general whole-school policies to support and extend achievement;

    ii.   identifying specific whole-school policies to combat underachievement;

    iii.   improving classroom practice.

● **Concerns for the future**

    i.   The need for more nursery places, not more 4 year olds in reception classes.

    ii.   The need for greater collaboration between primary and secondary schools.

iii. The need to recruit and retain quality teachers.

iv. The need to be aware that labelling children as level 1, level 2 or perhaps level 3 could in turn lower expectations and lead to levelling down rather than levelling up.

Managing Access and Entitlement in Primary Education

Managing access and entitlement in primary education is a major challenge. This paper endeavours to unpack some of the issues underlying this challenge and to identify strategies for future action.

A useful starting point is to ask two questions:

- access and entitlement for whom?
- access and entitlement to what?

There appears to be no difficulty in answering the first question whereas the answer to the second is not nearly so straightforward.

Access and entitlement for whom?

As far as access and entitlement for whom is concerned, there is common agreement that it is for the individual child — in other words — the learner. Back in the 1960s the Plowden Report's powerful opening statement, 'At the heart of the educational process lies the child', (C.A.C.E, 1967) made this point well. Twenty years later the Education Reform Act 1988 has reiterated this fundamental principle. It lays great stress on the notion of access and entitlement for all pupils. The concern that arose following the provision in the Act for disapplication and modification, was an example of the strength of feeling about the rights of each child to have access to all the learning opportunities to be provided by the school.

Access and entitlement to what?

When it comes to a consideration of the second question — access and entitlement to what? — the answer is not so clear cut and will be determined, for example, by notions of what is meant by 'good primary practice', views about the nature of teaching and learning, and definitions of the curriculum. The core issue when seeking an answer to this question centres around a long-running debate in primary education about process versus content.

The Plowden Report fuelled the debate and in subsequent years attention focused on the learning process and the need to develop classroom practice that:

(i) enables children to learn how to learn and so become autonomous learners;

(ii) emphasises active learning and the value of a wide range of real experiences that have meaning and relevance for children; and,

(iii) nurtures motivation and confidence and so supports the social, emotional and physical development of children as well as their intellectual development.

The importance of an entitlement to a wide range of learning opportunities was confirmed by HM Inspectorate's Primary Education in England (DES, 1978). The Inspectorate observed that a broad, as opposed to a narrow curriculum, supported pupil progress and attainment. However,HMI also raised issues about the content of the curriculum. In the findings, emphasis was placed on the need to ensure match, balance, continuity and progression in the curriculum on offer.

At the time of the Inspectorate's survey, 'good primary practice' was still synonymous with a process model. The process versus the content debate had encouraged a polarisation of views, and had perpetuated a divide between primary and secondary education, the latter being perceived as largely content-based.

In reality there was evidence in the HMI survey that primary education was still a lottery for children. Despite warnings by critics about the spread of 'progressive education', the process model was not in widespread use and the curriculum on offer was variable because there was no explicit agreement about the knowledge, skills and understanding children were entitled to have access to. The implication in the survey was that for some children school was an exciting, challenging place to be and offered a broad range of curriculum experiences. For others there was simply boredom because of the narrow, inappropriate curriculum on offer. In addition, the lottery was not just between schools but could also be found from class to class within the same school.

The impact of the 'Great Debate' initiated in the 1970s is well documented (Richards, 1984; Thomas, 1991). For the purpose of this paper, two milestones are worth recalling. The first is the publication of *The School Curriculum* (DES, 1981). The opening sentence was seemingly at odds with the prevailing view of primary education. It stated that, 'The school curriculum is at the heart of education.' This publication led to the requirement for LEAs to produce curriculum policy statements. The notion of good primary practice broadened to include the development and use of whole-school curriculum policies within schools to guide and support the work of teachers in the classroom.

The second milestone on the way to redefining good primary practice, is the publication of Section 1 of the Education Reform Act which deals with the National Curriculum. The act introduced a major policy change in relation to pupil entitlement. For the first time it spelt out the rights of all pupils in relation to the content of the curriculum. The Act made it quite clear that every pupil must have access to a curriculum which is 'balanced and broadly based' and general criteria were spelt out which were seen as 'an entitlement for all pupils.' (DES, 1989a). There were those who saw this as a threat to 'good primary practice' and claimed it was a secondary model that was being imposed on primary schools. However, once the dust settled and the non-statutory guidance began to emerge (NCC, 1989), teachers found that on the whole it combined approaches to learning, (for example, Attainment Targets 1 and 9 in mathematics and Attainment Target 1 in science), with subject knowledge and ideas in such a way as to provide class teachers with a much needed curriculum content framework. No longer did primary teachers have to invent the curriculum.

To try and separate curriculum content from the process of learning is to miss a fundamental point about access and entitlement. The need for children to acquire 'basic skills' to enable them to take advantage of educational opportunities has been well argued (Dearden, 1976). So too has the view that to become an autonomous learner capable of making informed choices, a child needs access to knowledge and understanding across the full range of human experience (Peters, 1966; Entwistle, 1978). How the curriculum is taught is seen as equally important, as this will determine the extent to which children are able to turn school knowledge into 'action knowledge' (Barnes, 1970) so making it their own and using it for their own purposes to increase their power as learners and exercise growing control over their own futures. In the light of such imperatives, arguments about process versus content in primary education are redundant and meaningless. Both are essential. Attention needs to focus instead on the quality of the match — the meeting point — between the two in the classroom. It is the extent of the match or mismatch between the learning process and the content to be learnt that will determine not just the quality of primary education on offer for the child, but also the equality of opportunity for each child to learn. The teaching methods used by the teacher to ensure this match are all important, — a point emphasised in the recent discussion paper on primary practice published by the DES (1992).

Under the new legislation the 'what' — the content — is, on the whole, controlled centrally. The 'how' — the process — is in the control of teachers. The underlying assumption is that by prescribing the content and linking it with statutory assessment arrangements, the lottery will be reduced and standards will rise. By legislating for access and entitlement it is anticipated that achievement levels for all will not only be set but hopefully will also be raised. Thus issues of access and entitlement have been made explicit and, for the first time, will be managed.

The lessons of research

So far so good, but an examination of research evidence raises serious questions about the in-built assumptions in the new legislation. The evidence available makes it clear that access and entitlement will not be managed unless it is managed by those who have the power to act. Three major lessons can be learnt from the research literature.

1. The link between disadvantage and achievement

There is ample research evidence to show that socio-economic inequality is a powerful determinant of differences in cognitive and educational attainment in children (ILEA, 1983, Mortimore and Mortimore, 1986). Social class, along with ethnic background, gender and disability, exerts a considerable influence on the life chances of young people.

Longitudinal studies provide a rich source of information about the link between pupils' background and their progress and attainment in school. An early study was published in the 1960s (Douglas, 1964). For a period of ten years it followed the progress of all the children born in the same week in March 1946. Using the Registrar General's categories for social class, the research found that for middle class children the combination of home and school experience led to improvements in progress and attainment. For children from working class families who were already coming to school disadvantaged compared with their middle class peer group, the school did not make up that disadvantage and by age 8 considerable differences in school performance, particularly with regard to reading were found. When the cohort was re-tested at 11 the differences had increased. However, it was found that whilst it was difficult to separate out the significance of the influence of home and school, there was evidence to show that in the schools with 'a good academic record', children from working class as well as middle class backgrounds were academically successful. The implication was that if a school was a 'good' school, then this could have a more significant influence on achievement than home background. This led the researchers to raise questions about how to prevent the 'wastage of the pool of talent in schools' and whether nursery education could be one answer to the problem.

The National Child Development Study (Davie *et al*, 1972) also found significant class differences in attainment. Children from social class category 5 (unskilled), for example, were found to have five times more reading problems at age 7, than children in category 1 (professional and managerial), with the difference doubling by age 11. Similarly, although to a lesser degree, differences in attainment in mathematics were also found between the two groups, with, as in reading, the gap widening at age 11. The next follow-up study of the cohort found that by age 16 three quarters of the children in category 5 had reading and mathematics scores that were below average (Essen and Wedge, 1982). The Child Health and Education Study (Osborn and Milbank, 1987) repeated these findings and provided further evidence that at age 10 the most socially disadvantaged children were significantly behind in their reading compared with those who were most advantaged. The APU surveys simply confirmed the results of earlier studies and, to take one example, following the survey of the mathematics performance of 10 year olds, showed that the differences in results between groups of pupils were related to social background factors (APU, 1980).

The Junior School Project, a longitudinal study of a cohort of junior aged children in London, proved to be an even more valuable source of evidence about the link between disadvantage and achievement (Mortimore, *et al*, 1988). This sophisticated study drew together what had previously been studied as separate aspects of disadvantage. It was able to map pupil progress and attainment across the dimensions of class, ethnicity, sex and age. The research revealed significant differences in children's educational outcomes during the junior years. Age, social class, sex and race were each found to have an impact on cognitive achievement levels at age 7 and 11. For example, children's level of reading attainment at 7 was a good predictor of their level of attainment at age 11. At 7, those children whose parents worked in non-manual jobs were nearly 10 months ahead in reading than pupils from unskilled manual homes. By the end of the third year, the gap had widened. It was also found that with non-cognitive outcomes such as behaviour and self-concept, there were differences according to age, social class, sex and race, although these differences did not necessarily correspond to the differences recorded in cognitive outcome. Overall, the project found that of age, sex, race and social class, it was the social class dimension that accounted for the main difference in attainment between groups of pupils.

Other studies have revealed a pattern of ethnic differences in attainment, with children from certain ethnic groups, for example, some of the Asian groups, achieving similar or better results than white British children. However, there is a tendency for other groups, in particular children of Afro-Caribbean origin, consistently to underachieve (Mabey, 1981).

The most recent longitudinal study has added a much needed dimension to the literature in terms of the age group studied (Tizard *et al*, 1988). Children aged 4 to 7 in a cohort of London schools were the focus of the study. The purpose of the research was to examine factors in the home and in the school that affect attainment and progress in the infant school. Particular attention was paid to the different levels of attainment of boys and girls and white British children and black British children of Afro-Caribbean origin. As with the Mortimore study the team found that there was a link between attainment and progress and that the literacy and numeracy knowledge and skills children had acquired before they started school were a strong predictor of attainment at age 7.

It is understandable, given the constraints of research and the tests available, that school achievement in the context of the studies described was mainly confined to progress and attainment in reading and mathematics. Some of the studies did examine other facets of achievement; for example, the Junior School Project examined a range of both cognitive and non-cognitive factors. In the day-to-day context within which adults and children work together in school, it is important to clarify what is understood by achievement. Assessing pupil progress and attainment along a narrow set of dimensions will give only a partial picture of an individual child and the effectiveness of a school as a whole.

A study of secondary education in the ILEA has provided a useful definition of achievement (Hargreaves *et al*, 1984). Four aspects of achievement were defined:

- acquisition of knowledge
- practical application of knowledge
- personal and social skills
- motivation and commitment.

These provide a broad frame of reference into which assessment about specific aspects of achievement can be incorporated as the teacher builds up a more general picture of the learner. The definition acts as a strong reminder that personal and social development is integral to a discussion about achievement. It also highlights the importance of the motivation of the learner, without which the chances of achieving successfully along the other three dimensions are considerably diminished. It was hardly surprising that a subsequent study of primary education in the ILEA (Thomas *et al*, 1985) adopted the same definition.

In relation to all four aspects, and there are no doubt others that could be added to the list, the school has a major contribution to make in raising levels of achievement. Whilst Bernstein (1970) gave a powerful reminder that 'Education cannot compensate for society', there is a growing amount of research evidence to demonstrate that, despite background factors, schools can and do enhance the achievement of pupils and that some schools are much more effective than others at doing so.

2. Schools matter

The Junior School Project was an important milestone in research into effective schooling in primary schools. The research team asked the following questions:

- 'Are some schools or classes more effective than others?

- Are some schools or classes more effective for particular groups of children?

- If some schools or classes are more effective than others, what factors contribute to these positive effects?'

Through the use of sophisticated research techniques the team was able to take account of background factors such as home language, family circumstances, age and sex. Account was also taken of factors within the school that are 'givens' such as size and the stability of staffing. By doing this the research team was able to focus on the factors controlled by the school such as teaching methods, record keeping and curriculum leadership, and examine which of these factors have a positive impact on pupil progress and attainment. It was the focus on progress that revealed the significance of schooling. For example, with reading the school effect was four times more important than home background. For mathematics and writing it was ten times. It was also the focus on progress that demonstrated that some schools are far more effective than others. Again with reading, for example, the average child in the most effective school increased his or her score on a 100 point reading test, by 25 points more than the average child attending the least effective school. The team found that schools which did better on one measure of academic progress, tended to do better on others (although there were exceptions) and that effective schools tended to be effective for all pupils despite social class, ethnic group, sex or age.

The research team identified 12 key factors that were consistently related to effective junior schooling. All the factors were ones that the head and staff could control and do something about. The factors ranged from 'the purposeful leadership of the staff by the headteacher', 'consistency amongst teachers', 'intellectually challenging teaching' through to 'parental involvement' and the creation of a 'positive climate'. Whilst the research team found that effective schools can and do 'jack-up' the achievement levels of all the children, they found that despite this what did not happen was a narrowing of the gap between the achievement levels of the disadvantaged and privileged groups.

The Tizard study (Tizard *et al.*, 1988) also found that school factors exerted a bigger influence on progress than home background. They found there were two major school factors associated with progress. The range of literacy and numeracy taught to the children and teachers' expectations. To a lesser extent, the particular school a child attended was linked with progress. Whilst each of these factors was independently associated with progress, the team found that the school a child attended proved to be an overriding factor in terms of the amount of progress a child made. In the case of reading the reception year in particular proved to be significant. Also, a relationship was found between teacher expectation and the range of curriculum opportunities provided for children especially in the areas of literacy and numeracy. The team reported that 'of the school-based measures we looked at, we found that teachers' academic expectations and children's curriculum coverage showed the strongest and most consistent association with school progress'. This finding is a cause for particular concern given the structure of the National Curriculum and the Assessment arrangements.

There are two other research studies that make an important contribution to an examination of school effectiveness and the extent to which schooling can not only 'jack-up' achievement for all but override disadvantage by narrowing the gap between the lowest and highest achieving groups. The first is the study by Osborn and Milbank (1987) already referred to. This study found that children who attended pre-school institutions achieved higher test scores at age 5 and 10 than children who had no pre-school experience. Out of the seven tests given, children who had no pre-school experience achieved the lowest score on four out of seven and the second lowest score in the other three. Advantaged children in private playgroups scored the highest with children who attended nursery schools a close second. It was the nursery school that catered mainly for working class children. However, of the most advantaged children 46% received no form of early years provision compared with only 10% of the most disadvantaged group. A further concern was that placing four year olds in reception classes in primary schools did not result in measurable improvements in achievement. In fact these children did no better than children who started school after their fifth birthday, and had had no pre-school experience.

The value of nursery education for disadvantaged children was an important finding of this study. A more recent study (Athey, 1990) supports the findings of Osborn and Milbank and provides a wealth of data to show that not only is it possible for teachers to improve the achievement levels of children from disadvantaged socio-economic backgrounds, but it is also possible to narrow the gap in levels of achievement between working class and middle class children. The study was a five year 'Early Education Project' that focused on ways of extending young children's thinking in the 3 to 5 age group. Two groups of children were studied closely: an experimental group comprised of children from socio-economic groups 4 and 5 and a comparison group of children from Registrar General's category 1. The involvement of parents was an integral part of the research.

On initial testing the experimental group were significantly behind the comparison group on all the tests given. At the end of the programme the group had made highly significant gains in test scores so reducing the gap between themselves and the comparison group. Two years later the children were tested again and the progress made had been sustained. Older siblings of children in the experimental group were also tested as part of the research. At the beginning the scores were similar, at the end older siblings were lagging noticeably behind. For example, 'after two years in primary school the experimental group were six months ahead of their chronological age on 'accuracy' of reading, and three months ahead on their chronological age on 'comprehension' of reading. On the same tests the older siblings 'lagged' one year and two months behind their chronological age.'

The reason for the gains, Athey argues, was the quality of curriculum content provided by the teacher and supported by the parents. By observing children at work and listening to what they had to say the teacher was able to identify their current pattern of thinking and provide a rich range of curriculum experiences to support and extend the children's conceptual development. The quality of the match — the meeting point between the methods used, the content and the learning process — determined the degree of progress. The research argues against deficit views of working class children by demonstrating how the curriculum choices made by teachers can and do affect progress and attainment. The summative results of the project show that initial wide differentiation in cognitive functioning can be reduced by early education. The research confirms the importance of day-to-day formative assessment of progress to determine the next step for the child as opposed to summative assessment being the deciding factor in curriculum planning. In addition this project demonstrates how parents can become real partners in raising achievement. Other studies have highlighted the importance of communication about learning between teachers and parents (Tizard, Mortimore and Burchell, 1981) and that parents do want to help with their child's education (Tizard *et al*, 1988). A useful review of international research findings in relation to how parents can become active rather than silent partners in the education of their children has been provided by Wallace and Walberg (1991).

All these researchers combine to demonstrate the importance of schooling. Heads and class teachers can understandably feel relieved that the time and effort that goes into preparing, delivering and assessing the range of curriculum experiences offered to, and received by children, can and does make a highly significant impact on children's progress and attainment. The challenge of how to improve the quality of teaching and learning is not a new one. Nor is the recognition that it is important to be aware that under-achievement is not just a phenomenon of working class children or certain ethnic groups. It can occur for any pupil regardless of background. It would of course be unrealistic to expect all pupils to achieve the same level of attainment and to make the same progress. Nevertheless, whole groups should not underachieve.

3.   Test results can be unreliable

It is important to recognise that test results can be unreliable and cannot provide a full picture of the effectiveness of a particular school. The work of Nuttall and Goldstein (1989a) in relation to secondary examination results has lessons for primary education. Through sophisticated multi-level analysis they have shown that the aggregate examination results for a school can mask variations in individual and group progress and attainment. Their research makes it clear that test results cannot be used to predict or represent the real academic chances of pupils. Given the reporting requirements of the National Curriculum this is a significant finding. For example they have found that a school's overall examination results may be satisfactory or good when in reality a close scrutiny reveals that certain groups are in fact not making satisfactory or good progress; instead they are underachieving. In other words a school might appear, because of its examination results, to be an effective school, and given research findings about effective schools, it may be assumed that all pupils are receiving an effective education when in fact this is not the case. The opposite is also possible, namely that a school may appear to have unsatisfactory results overall when a close examination may reveal that given the intake and taking account of other 'given' factors as the Junior School Project did, the school is in fact improving pupil progress and for some groups of pupils enabling them to achieve higher attainment levels than expected. Nuttall and Goldstein also found that the effectiveness of a school varies along several dimensions; in other words a school may be very effective in one aspect of its work but less so in others, and variations can occur from year to year. The message from this research is that a single measure of effectiveness is misleading.

The Junior School Project illustrated these points well and provided powerful evidence for the need to focus on rates of progress rather than summative snapshots. It is the extent to which a school provides access to the knowledge and experiences children are entitled to and the consequent improvements in learning that children make, that should be the deciding factor as to whether or not a school is effectively offering equality of educational opportunity. The value added by the school is a crucial factor (Nuttall and Goldstein, 1989b).

Managing Access and Entitlement — Practical Implications

It might be helpful to review what has been said so far in this paper about managing access and entitlement in primary education.

1.   The process and content of learning are vital factors in ensuring equality of opportunity. It is the quality of these opportunities that determines levels of achievement. The role of the teacher is central as it is the teacher in the classroom who decides how best to match the curriculum to the learner. Parents themselves also have a role to play.

2.   There is a link between disadvantage and underachievement which can affect children's life chances and influence teachers' expectations of children's capacity to learn.

3.   Schools matter. They can improve progress and so raise the achievement levels of all the children in a school. They can further help to combat disadvantage by narrowing the difference between the highest and the lowest achieving groups. Good quality early years education has a vital role to play.

4.   Improving achievement levels of children regardless of background factors is very complex. Assessing the effectiveness of a school on test results alone can mask the reality for individuals and groups. Complacency or unwarranted criticism could ensue.

5.   Managing access and entitlement is essential, because it will not happen by chance.

This paper has argued that to achieve access and entitlement requires good management. It has also used research evidence to demonstrate that essentially it is the schools themselves that have it within their control to make a major impact on levels of achievement. Schools do not improve simply because of new legislation and because of LEA policy. They do not improve simply because an inspector or an advisory teacher comes to call. They can and do improve substantially as a result of the actions taken by those who work within them. It is the will to improve and the quality and expertise of the staff that are so important.

It is heads and teachers who have shown what is possible and the findings of the Junior School Project illustrate this quite dramatically. The National Curriculum has made a significant contribution but it will be the schools themselves that will determine the success of its implementation. At the end of the day the evidence of research points to the fact that it is the quality of the leadership provided by the headteacher that can be, and so often is, the overriding factor in school effectiveness (Thomas, 1985; Nias and Southworth, 1992). Nevertheless schools cannot do it alone. The responsibility for raising levels of achievement by improving progress must be a collective one — a partnership for entitlement between those involved. A partnership between teacher and child; between class teacher and the head and other colleagues on the staff; between the home and school; between the school and the LEA; between the LEA and Central Government. LMS has strengthened the role of the school in this partnership but to fulfil this increased responsibility schools need a good quality service from those with responsibility beyond the school gate. The teacher and child in the classroom must ultimately be the focus of the partnership. Each of the partners involved will have different roles to play but they share the same task — to assure quality — to provide access and entitlement for all. To make the partnership work there needs to be openness and trust and a commitment to translating policy into practice in such a way that children really are 'at the heart of the educational process'.

Managing Access and Entitlement — Practical Strategies for Schools

Managing access and entitlement requires heads and teachers to have a clear idea about: what it is they want to achieve; how well they are doing at present; what needs to be done next. Any discussions about policy and practice in school need to be informed by general principles that are shared by all the staff. For example, it is important for a school to be explicit about how children best learn and to define achievement. The school's general view about the curriculum also needs to be made clear. No less important is the school's view about equal opportunities. The kinds of progress and performance indicators to be used and the evidence of progress and performance the school intends to collect and share with children, parents, governors and others need to be decided. Both qualitative and quantitative data will be important.

Once general principles have been clarified the task of managing access and entitlement can be approached in three different ways although in practice the three are interdependent.

1. Establishing general whole-school policies to support and extend achievement.

At the level of the whole school it is possible to identify which factors in the school have an impact on achievement and require a policy that everyone agrees to put into practice. The Junior School Project is just one example of how a school can be helped to achieve this. The research identified 12 key factors that relate to effectiveness. By using these as an aide-memoire a school can soon assess how well it is doing and what needs to be improved. Record keeping, for example, was one of the factors. It may well be that a school decides to broaden the present system so that it becomes a record of achievement that is contributed to and shared by children and parents.

2. Identifying specific whole-school policies to combat under-achievement

In recognition of the research evidence that whilst an effective school can raise achievement levels in general, groups and individuals may well be underachieving, a school can identify very practical steps that can be taken to address this key issue. These might include:

i.   rigorous monitoring and review of the progress of specific individuals and groups who could be vulnerable, for example, bilingual learners, summer born children, children with disabilities, children from certain social and ethnic backgrounds;

ii.   early identification of underachievement and the establishment of a detailed action plan for improvement for each child concerned;

iii. close scrutiny of resources to ensure they are appropriate for all pupils and do not contain damaging stereotypes or materials that disadvantage some children;

iv.   combatting potential low expectations of teachers and other adults in the school through moderation activities, inservice education courses, visits to other schools;

v.   planned use of adults other than the classteacher within the school and good communication about children's progress.

3. Improving classroom practice

It should go without saying that the acid test of any policy is the extent to which it can be seen in action in the classroom and the impact it is making on the progress of individual learners. Policy established at the level of the whole school needs to be translated into practical, manageable steps that support and guide the work of teachers in the classroom.

In a paper such as this it is not possible to cite all the practical strategies a teacher can adopt to ensure access and entitlement for each child. Research evidence and HMI reports drawn from direct observation of teachers in classrooms have identified many of the essential elements of good practice (DES, 1987). Elements such as curriculum planning, assessment, record keeping, classroom talk, management and organisation, and expectations and relationships have been reported on in detail. When considering these and others, all important is the quality of the day-to-day decisions a teacher takes in relation to the next learning step for a child. The key role of the teacher in matching the process and the content of learning has already been examined. The National Curriculum and assessment requirements have raised the profile of teacher assessment. Much good can come of this providing improved planning and assessment go hand in hand. Improving a teacher's ability to identify what children can do and can go on to learn next is at the hub of teaching and learning. Practical steps such as helping children to set manageable targets, making explicit the achievements expected and collecting evidence of that achievement can all contribute to improving progress and attainment.

Managing access and entitlement at these three levels will require a systematic approach to school improvement by the head and staff. The processes of development planning outlined in the DES publications (DES, 1989b, 1991) provide a systematic approach to improvement and enable schools to set themselves realistic and achievable targets. The LEA has an important role in supporting the school in this process. It is essential that, just as teachers need to establish a range of strategies to ensure effective learning in the classroom, the LEA also should establish strategies for helping schools to make themselves more effective. Shared performance indicators, shared monitoring and assessment and quality inservice training can all make an important contribution.

Future Concerns

In the context of access and entitlement it is worth raising four particular concerns for the future.

1. The need for more nursery places

The importance of the early years has been identified in this paper, yet a commitment to provide nursery places for all who need them is not forthcoming. The financial constraints facing LEAs at present place what nursery education there is at risk.

2. The need to break down phase barriers

Primary and secondary schools need to collaborate much more in the future. The National Curriculum makes this even more urgent. Primary education can no longer be perceived as simply a preparation for secondary school. It is of vital importance in its own right and if continuity and progression are to be assured then good communication between schools will be essential. It is also the case that primary teachers lack curriculum subject expertise in several areas, (DES, 1992) which is understandable. Secondary schools have that expertise and ways need to be found to share it with primary colleagues. Primary teachers have a good knowledge of classroom practice and in turn can assist secondary teachers with mixed ability teaching.

3. The need to recruit and retain quality teachers

Initial training and inservice training are key factors in enhancing the professionalism of teachers. Access and entitlement requires good teachers. Good teachers will not come into the profession or remain in it unless they are valued, supported and given positive encouragement to improve.

4. Levelling — down or up?

Not all children can achieve the same educational level. However there is a potential danger in the national assessment arrangements that have been put in place. The requirement to allocate each child to a level and so label a child, for example, as level 1, level 2 or level 3 could result in teachers teaching to the level and grouping children accordingly. This in turn could lower teachers' expectations and in the longer term lead to levelling down as opposed to levelling up. The very principles of entitlement written into the National Curriculum could be defeated. A powerful statement by Entwistle (1978) acts as a sharp reminder of the need to avoid such a scenario at all costs.

> 'Though notions of educational ceilings (i.e. absolute limits on anyone's development) may be useful in certain contexts, the likelihood is that these are usually a good deal higher for most people than elitist educational theorists are apt to suppose. For their own good reasons (if only to survive in an unpromising social environment) individuals may build their own cognitive ceilings very low, opting for an anti-intellectual, cognitively impoverished stance on life. But no one has the right to be architect of anyone else's low-ceilinged educational hovel, and the existence of late developers who break through the educational roof is all the justification necessary for the view that for anyone, educationally, only the sky is the limit. For once the possibility of rationality and critical awareness is allowed in relation to any of life's enterprises, there can be no guarantee that the germ of rationality in any life can be sterilised once it has begun to fructify.'

References

APU (1980), *Mathematical Development Primary Survey,* HMSO, London.

Athey, C. (1990), *Extending Thought in Young Children,* Paul Chapman, London.

Barnes, D. (1976), *From Communication to Curriculum,* Penguin, Harmondsworth.

Bernstein, B. (1970), *'Education Cannot Compensate for Society',* New Society 387.

Central Advisory Council for Education, (1967), *Children and their Primary Schools* (the Plowden Report), HMSO, London.

Davie, R. *et al,* (1972), *From Birth to Seven,* Longman, Harlow.

Dearden, R. (1976), *Problems in Primary Education,* Routledge, London.

DES (1978), *Primary Education in England,* HMSO, London.

DES (1981), *The School Curriculum,* HMSO, London.

DES (1987), *Primary Schools: Some Aspects of Good Practice*, HMSO, London.

DES (1988), *The Education Reform Act,* Chapter 1, Part 1, HMSO, London.

DES (1989a), *National Curriculum: From Policy to Practice,* HMSO, London.

DES (1989b) *Planning for School Development,* HMSO, London.

DES (1991) Development Planning: A Practical Guide., HMSO, London.

DES (1992) *Curriculum Organisation and Classroom Practice in Primary Schools,* HMSO, London.

Douglas, J.W.B. (1964), *The Home and School,* Macgibbon & Kee, London.

Entwistle, H. (1978), *Class Culture and Education,* Methuen, London.

Essen, J. & Wedge, P. (1982), *Continuities in Childhood Disadvantage,* Heinemann, London.

Hargreaves, D. *et al,* (1984), *Improving Secondary Schools,* ILEA, London.

ILEA, (1983), *Race, Sex and Class 1. Achievement in Schools,* ILEA, London.

Mabey, C. (1981), *Black British Literacy: A Study of Reading Attainment of London Black Children from 8 to 15 years*, ILEA, London.

Mortimore, P. and Mortimore, J. (1986), *Education and Social Class,* in Rogers, R., (ed.) *Education and Social Class,* (1986), Falmer, Lewes.

Mortimore, P. *et al,* (1988), *School Matters,* Open Books, Wells.

National Curriculum Council (1989), *Mathematics Non-Statutory Guidance* and *Science Non-Statutory Guidance,* NCC, York.

Nias, J. and Southworth, G. (1992), *Whole School Curriculum Development in the Primary School,* Falmer, Lewes.

Nuttall, D. Goldstein, H. *et al,* (1989a), 'Differential School Effectiveness', *International Journal of Educational Research,* Vol.13, pp.769-776.

Nuttall, D. Goldstein, H. (1989b) 'Finely Measured Gains: 'value-added' approach to measuring school effectiveness'. *TES,* Oct.17, 1989, p.14.

Osborn, A.F. and Milbank, J.E. (1987), *The Effects of Early Education,* Clarendon Press, Oxford.

Peters, R.S. (1966), *Ethics and Education,* Allen & Unwin London.

Richards, C. (1984), *The Study of Primary Education,* Falmer Press, Lewes.

Thomas, N. *et al,* (1985), *Improving Primary Schools,* ILEA, London.

Thomas, N. (1991), *Primary Education from Plowden to the 1990s,* Falmer, Lewes.

Tizard, B. Mortimore, J. & Burchell, B. (1981). *Involving Parents in Nursery and Infant Schools,* Grant McIntyre, London.

Tizard, B. *et al,* (1988), *Young Children at School in the Inner City,* Lawrence Erlbaum Associations, New York.

Wallace, T. & Walberg, H.J. (1991), 'Parental Partnerships for Learning', *International Journal of Educational Research,* Vol.15, No.2. pp.131-144.

ASPE

Association for the Study of Primary Education

A national body committed to the advancement of primary education through collaborative study and action

ASPE aims to promote:

productive professional collaboration
the advancement of understanding
the enhancement of practice
dissemination of information
independent and informed commentary on major issues

Membership Secretary:

Janet Wellings, Education Department, Shire Hall, Raingate Street, Bury St Edmunds IP33 2AR

Background

ASPE was founded in the belief that one of the best ways to advance the cause of primary education, and to help those most directly involved, is through collaborative study.

Why study? The word perhaps needs to be freed of its more arid overtones. To study, simply, is to apply the mind in order to learn and understand. Study, therefore, is not the sole property of particular groups or institutions but can be undertaken by anyone, anywhere. It can also take many forms, ranging from the 'pure' study of broad issues and purposes to the 'applied' tackling of very specific practical problems. We all need to learn and to understand in order to enhance our practice, so study in this comprehensive sense is a basic professional pursuit.

Why collaboration? The child and the teacher are at the centre of primary education. But they need sustaining — by fellow-teachers, by heads, by parents, by advisers, by teacher educators, by researchers, by administrators, by governors, and so on. Each of these groups can claim to be in the business, one way or another, of supporting primary education. Yet frequently they may work in isolation from one another. Too often, indeed, this separateness may lead to mutual misunderstanding and even misrepresentation. Yet they all have something valuable and distinctive to offer.

Collaborative study of primary education harnesses the potential of each of these groups in the context of shared concerns and challenges. Mutual support and co-operation benefit everyone, but most of all the child.

Following an exploratory meeting in Warwick in 1987, the Association for the Study of Primary Education — ASPE — was launched in September 1988 at a national conference held in Leeds. A constitution was approved which reflects these basic principles, and a steering committee was elected to plan the first year's programme. ASPE is now in its fourth year, building on the success of the first three.

Membership of ASPE is open to all involved in primary education. The founding conference had strong and balanced representation from class teachers, heads, advisers and inspectors, teacher educators and researchers, as well as from other groups. ASPE's success as a force within and on behalf of primary education will depend in large measure on maintaining this balance of professional perspective. At the same time, because the classroom is at the hub of primary education, we are particularly keen to have strong representation from class teachers.

Activities

ASPE operates at two levels, national and regional/local.

NATIONAL ACTIVITIES include: major conferences (national conferences have so far been held in Leeds, Bristol, Dudley and Cambridge), liaison with other national primary organisations and groups, with LEAs and HMI, and with DES, NCC, SEAC and other official bodies; production and dissemination of papers, reports and responses both to targeted bodies and through in-house and established publications.